CULTIVATING SELF-DISCIPLINE

SECRETS METHODS FOR ACHIEVING YOUR GOALS

DR. JAGADEESH PILLAI

Made with ♥ on the Notion Press Platform
www.notionpress.com

|| Dedicated to all wisdom seekers around the world ||

ꕥ

Contents

Contents

Prayer

"Om Bhadram Karnebhih Shrunuyaama DevaahBhadram Pashyemaakshabhiryajatraah SthirairangaistushtuvaamsastanoobhihVyashema Devahitam YadaayuhSwasti Na Indro VridhashravaahSwasti Nah Pooshaa VishwavedaahSwasti Nastaarkshyo ArishtanemihSwasti No Brihaspatir DadhaatuOm Shantih, Shantih, Shantih"

The literal meaning of this mantra is: OM. O Gods! Let us hear auspicious words from our ears. O reverent Gods! Let us behold propitious visions from our eyes, let our organs and body be stable, healthy, and strong. Let us do that which is pleasing to the gods in the life span allotted to us. May Indra, inscribed in the scriptures, bring us fortune! May Pushan, the knower of the world, grant us prosperity! May Trakshya, who vanquishes enemies, bestow us with blessings! May Brihaspati bring us success!
OM Peace, Peace, Peace.

About The Author

Dr. Jagadeesh Pillai is a renowned Guinness World Record holder, writer, and researcher hailing from Varanasi, also known as the abode of Lord Shiva. With a Ph.D. in Vedic Science and a range of creative ideas and achievements, he is a true polymath. He is the author of more than 100 books including Research Publications. Although his roots can be traced back to Kerala, the people of Varanasi hold him in high regard and affectionately consider him one of their own.

In 1998, Dr. Pillai was offered a job at Banaras Hindu University, but he left the position after only two months to pursue greater goals in life. He believed that in order to study Indian scriptures and engage in other creative endeavours, he needed to retire from the daily grind of working solely for money at a young age.

He started an export business from scratch, using the knowledge he had gained from a previous job in the industry. His intelligence and unique approach to business led to great success in a short period of time, earning him more in just a decade and a half than he would have in a lifetime working in a government job. Upon the passing of Dr. APJ Abdul Kalam, Dr. Pillai decided to leave the business and dedicate himself to reading, studying, researching, and experimenting.

During his tenure in the export business, Dr. Pillai traveled to over 16 countries, gaining valuable insight and experiencing the world and life in detail.

Dr. Pillai has achieved four Guinness World Records in the following subjects:

"Script to Screen" - In this record, Dr. Pillai produced and directed an animation film within the shortest time possible, breaking the previous record set by Canadians. He has also received numerous national and international awards and recognitions for this achievement.

Longest Line of Postcards - For this record, Dr. Pillai created a line of 16,300 postcards on the occasion of the 163rd anniversary of Indian Postal Day. The event also included a questionnaire about the Indian flag.

Largest Poster Awareness Campaign - Dr. Pillai designed an awareness campaign on the subject of "Beti Bachao - Beti Padhao" (Save the Girl Child - Educate the Girl Child) to achieve this record.

Largest Envelope - In tribute to the Indian Prime Minister's "Make in India" initiative, Dr. Pillai created a 4000 square meter envelope using waste paper to achieve this record.

Attempted - **70000 Candles on a 210 kg Cake** - To celebrate the 70th Indian Independence Day, Dr. Pillai attempted to light 70,000 candles on a 210 kg cake, which was recorded in World Records India.

Attempted - **Documentary on Dhamek Stupa of Sarnath in 17 Languages** - Dr. Pillai attempted to create a documentary on the Dhamek Stupa of Sarnath, dubbing it in 17 different languages. The result of this attempt is currently awaiting confirmation from the Guinness World Records.

Dr. Pillai is skilled in teaching the Bhagavad Gita, a Hindu scripture, and is popular among young people. He has helped many young people improve their lives through his motivational teachings.

In addition to teaching, he has composed and sung numerous Sanskrit Bhajans and patriotic songs.

He has also written and directed several short films and documentaries for awareness campaigns, and has volunteered with the police in both UP and Kerala to spread awareness about various issues through videos and photography.

Incredibly, he has produced and directed over 100 documentaries about the city of Varanasi, all on his own.

He has also helped and guided more than 25 boys and girls to achieve world records through creative and innovative methods. He is a multifaceted person who uses his intellect and the blessings given to him by God to excel in various areas. He is both a teacher and a student, always learning and teaching, and is able to master any subject he comes across.

He is a selfless social activist and motivational speaker who has overcome struggles and failures to become a successful and enthusiastic individual with a rich life experience.

In addition to his work with the Bhagavad Gita, he is also an efficient Tarot card reader, Astro-Vastu consultant, and a talented singer and composer. He has sung the entire Ram Charita Manas and Bhagavad Gita in his own compositions, and has sung the phrase "Lokah Samastha Sukhino Bhavantu" in 50 different languages. He is currently working on a detailed and scientific study of Vedas, Upanishads, Puranas, and the Bhagavad Gita. He has also composed and sung the Hanuman Chalisa and Gayatri Mantra in 108 and 1008 different compositions, respectively.

Awards - Four Times Guinness World Records, Winner of Mahatma Gandhi Vishwa Shanti Puraskar, Mahatma Gandhi Global Peace Ambassador, Kashi Ratna Award, Dr. APJ Abdul Kalam Motivational Person of the Year 2017, Mother Teresa Award, Indira Gandhi Priyadarshini Award, Bharat Vikas Ratna Award, Udyog Ratna Award, Vigyan Prasar Award, Poorvanchal Ratn Samman.

Preface

In this book, "Cultivating Self-Discipline: Secrets Methods for Achieving Your Goals," we will explore the importance of self-discipline and how it can help you achieve your goals. Self-discipline is the ability to control oneself and make oneself do what needs to be done, and it is a vital trait for anyone who wants to achieve their goals and live a fulfilling life.

This book is for anyone who has ever struggled with following through on their commitments or for those who want to build their self-discipline to better handle the challenges that come their way. It is for those who want to learn the secret methods for cultivating self-discipline and achieving their goals.

We will cover a wide range of topics including setting SMART goals, creating a plan, building a daily routine, overcoming procrastination, staying motivated, building mental and physical strength, managing distractions, staying focused, understanding and overcoming resistance to change, building willpower and self-control, the power of positive thinking and gratitude, dealing with failure, learning from mistakes, building resilience and coping with setbacks, learning to adapt and be flexible, the role of mindfulness, the power of persistence and determination.

This book will provide you with the tools you need to cultivate self-discipline, achieve your goals, and live a fulfilling life. It is my hope that by reading this book, you will gain the understanding, knowledge, and confidence to take action and make your dreams a reality.

I

Introduction: Understanding Self-Discipline and Its Importance for Achieving Your Goals

In this chapter, we will explore the concept of self-discipline and its importance for achieving your goals. Self-discipline is the ability to control one's emotions, thoughts, and behaviors in order to achieve a desired outcome. It is a key factor in achieving success and reaching your goals.

Self-discipline is a skill that can be developed and strengthened over time. It requires practice and dedication to master. It is important to understand that self-discipline is not about being perfect or having superhuman willpower. It is about having the ability to make decisions and take action in order to reach your goals.

Self-discipline is essential for achieving success. It helps you stay focused and motivated, even when things get tough. It also helps you stay on track and make progress towards your goals. Self-discipline can help you stay organized and manage your time effectively. It can also help you stay disciplined in other areas of your life, such as diet and exercise.

Self-discipline is also important for developing good habits. Habits are the building blocks of success. They are the small, consistent actions that you take every day that lead to big results over time. Developing good habits requires self-discipline and consistency.

Finally, self-discipline is important for developing resilience. Resilience is the ability to bounce back from setbacks and keep going despite challenges. It is an essential skill for achieving success. Self-discipline helps you stay focused and motivated, even when things don't go as planned.

In conclusion, self-discipline is an essential skill for achieving success and reaching your goals. It requires practice and dedication to master, but it is a skill that can be developed and strengthened over time. Self-discipline helps you stay focused and motivated, develop good habits, and develop resilience. It is an invaluable tool for achieving your goals.

"Self-discipline is the bridge between goals and accomplishment."

- Jim Rohn

ꙮ

II

Setting SMART Goals and Creating a Plan

Writing effective goals is an essential part of cultivating self-discipline. Setting SMART goals and creating a plan to achieve them can help you stay focused and motivated on the path to success.

SMART stands for Specific, Measurable, Achievable, Relevant, and Time-bound. When setting goals, it is important to make sure they are specific and measurable. This will help you track your progress and stay on track. Additionally, make sure your goals are achievable and relevant to your overall objectives. Finally, set a timeline for yourself to ensure you stay on track and reach your goals in a timely manner.

Creating a plan to achieve your goals is also important.

Start by breaking down your goals into smaller, more manageable tasks. This will help you stay organized and focused on the steps you need to take to reach your goals. Additionally, create a timeline for yourself and set deadlines for each task. This will help you stay on track and motivated to reach your goals.

Finally, it is important to stay motivated and focused on your goals. Make sure to reward yourself for completing tasks and reaching milestones. This will help you stay motivated and on track. Additionally, it is important to stay organized and review your progress regularly. This will help you stay focused and make sure you are on track to reach your goals.

By setting SMART goals and creating a plan to achieve them, you can cultivate self-discipline and stay motivated on the path to success. With the right mindset and a clear plan, you can reach your goals and achieve success.

"Discipline is the foundation upon which all success is built."

III

Building a Daily Routine for Self-Discipline

Creating a daily routine for self-discipline is essential for achieving your goals. It can be difficult to stay motivated and focused on your goals, but having a daily routine can help you stay on track. Here are some tips for building a daily routine that will help you cultivate self-discipline:

1. Start your day with a plan. Before you begin your day, take a few moments to plan out what you want to accomplish. This will help you stay focused and motivated throughout the day.

2. Set realistic goals. It's important to set realistic goals that you can actually achieve. This will help you stay motivated and on track.

3. Break down tasks into smaller chunks. Breaking down tasks into smaller chunks can make them more manageable and easier to complete.

4. Prioritize tasks. Prioritizing tasks can help you stay focused and organized.

5. Take breaks. Taking regular breaks throughout the day can help you stay focused and energized.

6. Reward yourself. Rewarding yourself for completing tasks can help you stay motivated and on track.

Creating a daily routine for self-discipline is an important step in achieving your goals. By following these tips, you can create a routine that will help you stay focused and motivated. With a daily routine in place, you can cultivate self-discipline and reach your goals.

"The only discipline that lasts is self-discipline."

- B.C. Forbes

ꕥ

IV

Overcoming Procrastination and Staying Motivated

Procrastination is a common problem that can prevent us from reaching our goals, while staying motivated is key to staying on track.

The first step to overcoming procrastination is to identify the underlying cause. Is it fear of failure, lack of interest, or something else? Once you have identified the cause, you can begin to address it. For example, if you are afraid of failure, you can start by setting realistic goals and breaking them down into smaller, achievable tasks. This will help you to feel more confident and motivated.

Another way to overcome procrastination is to create a plan

of action. Make a list of tasks that need to be completed and set a timeline for each one. This will help you stay organized and focused on the task at hand. Additionally, it is important to reward yourself for completing tasks. This will help to keep you motivated and on track.

Finally, it is important to stay motivated. This can be done by setting short-term goals and celebrating small successes. Additionally, it is important to take breaks and give yourself time to relax. This will help to keep you energized and motivated.

By following these steps, you can overcome procrastination and stay motivated. With a little self-discipline and dedication, you can achieve your goals and cultivate a successful life.

"Self-discipline is the key to success; it unlocks the door to a world of possibilities."

ꕥ

V

Building Mental and Physical Strength

Mental and physical strength are both essential components of self-discipline, and both must be developed in order to reach one's goals.

Mentally, self-discipline requires a strong will and a clear focus on the desired outcome. To build mental strength, one must practice self-reflection and self-awareness. This means taking the time to reflect on one's thoughts and feelings, and to identify any negative patterns that may be holding them back. Additionally, it is important to set realistic goals and to break them down into achievable steps. This will help to keep motivation high and to stay on track.

Physically, self-discipline requires a healthy lifestyle. This includes eating a balanced diet, getting enough sleep, and exercising regularly. Eating a balanced diet will provide the body with the nutrients it needs to stay energized and focused. Getting enough sleep will help to keep the mind sharp and alert. And exercising regularly will help to build strength and endurance, which are essential for achieving one's goals.

In conclusion, building mental and physical strength is essential for cultivating self-discipline. To do this, one must practice self-reflection and self-awareness, set realistic goals, and maintain a healthy lifestyle. With dedication and perseverance, anyone can develop the mental and physical strength needed to reach their goals.

"Self-discipline is the ability to make yourself do what you should do, when you should do it, whether you feel like it or not."

VI

Managing Distractions and Staying Focused

Distractions can come in many forms, from the mundane to the extreme, and can be a major obstacle to success.

The first step in managing distractions is to identify them. This can be done by taking a few moments to reflect on what is causing the distraction. Is it a physical object, such as a phone or computer? Is it a person or situation? Once the source of the distraction is identified, it can be addressed.

The next step is to create a plan to manage the distraction. This could include setting boundaries, such as limiting the amount of time spent on a particular activity or setting a specific goal for the day. It could also include creating a distraction-free environment, such as turning off notifications or removing clutter from the workspace.

Finally, it is important to stay focused on the task at hand. This can be done by breaking down the task into smaller, more manageable chunks and setting a timer to stay on track. It can also be helpful to take regular breaks to give the mind a chance to rest and refocus.

Managing distractions and staying focused is an essential part of cultivating self-discipline and achieving goals. By taking the time to identify and address distractions, creating a plan to manage them, and staying focused on the task at hand, it is possible to stay on track and reach success.

"Self-discipline is the ability to do what needs to be done, even when you don't want to do it."

VII

Understanding and Overcoming Resistance to Change

This resistance can be both internal and external, and it can manifest in a variety of ways. It is important to understand the sources of resistance to change and to develop strategies for overcoming it.

Resistance to change can come from a variety of sources. It can be internal, such as fear of the unknown or a lack of self-confidence. It can also be external, such as a lack of support from family or friends, or a lack of resources. It is important to identify the source of resistance in order to develop an effective strategy for overcoming it.

One way to overcome resistance to change is to focus on the

positive aspects of the change. It is important to recognize the potential benefits of the change and to focus on those. This can help to reduce fear and anxiety and to motivate individuals to take action.

Another way to overcome resistance to change is to create a plan. It is important to break down the change into smaller, more manageable steps. This can help to reduce the feeling of being overwhelmed and can make the change seem more achievable.

Finally, it is important to be patient and to recognize that change takes time. It is important to be realistic about the timeline and to recognize that progress may be slow. It is also important to be flexible and to adjust the plan as needed.

Understanding and overcoming resistance to change is an important part of achieving goals. It is important to identify the sources of resistance and to develop strategies for overcoming it. By focusing on the positive aspects of the change, creating a plan, and being patient, individuals can successfully overcome resistance to change and achieve their goals.

"Self-discipline is the ability to control your emotions, thoughts, and behaviors in pursuit of your goals."

VIII

Building Willpower and Self-Control

Willpower and self-control are essential for achieving any goal. They are the foundation of self-discipline, and without them, it is impossible to make progress. Fortunately, these skills can be developed and strengthened with practice.

The first step to building willpower and self-control is to identify the areas where you need to improve. This could be anything from procrastination to unhealthy eating habits. Once you have identified the areas that need work, you can begin to develop strategies to help you stay on track.

One of the most effective strategies for building willpower and self-control is to set small, achievable goals. This will help you stay motivated and focused on the task at hand. Additionally, it is important to reward yourself for reaching each goal. This will help to reinforce the behavior and make it easier to stay on track.

Another important strategy for building willpower and self-control is to practice mindfulness. This involves being aware of your thoughts and feelings in the present moment. This will help you to stay focused on the task at hand and resist any distractions.

Finally, it is important to practice self-compassion. This means being kind to yourself when you make mistakes or fail to reach a goal. This will help to keep you motivated and prevent you from giving up.

By following these strategies, you can develop the willpower and self-control necessary to achieve your goals. With practice and dedication, you can cultivate the self-discipline needed to reach your highest potential.

"Self-discipline is the key to unlocking your inner strength and achieving success."

IX

The Power of Positive Thinking and Gratitude

Positive thinking and gratitude are two of the most powerful tools available to those seeking to cultivate self-discipline.

Positive thinking is the practice of focusing on the good in any situation. It is the act of looking for the silver lining in any cloud. It is the ability to see the potential in any challenge. Positive thinking is a powerful tool for self-discipline because it helps to keep us motivated and focused on our goals. When we focus on the positive, we are more likely to stay on track and take the necessary steps to achieve our goals.

Gratitude is another powerful tool for cultivating self-discipline. Gratitude is the practice of recognizing and appreciating the good in our lives. It is the act of being thankful for the blessings we have been given. Gratitude helps us to stay focused on our goals and to stay motivated. When we are grateful for what we have, we are more likely to take the necessary steps to achieve our goals.

Positive thinking and gratitude are two of the most powerful tools available to those seeking to cultivate self-discipline. By focusing on the positive and being grateful for what we have, we can stay motivated and focused on our goals. We can use these tools to help us stay on track and take the necessary steps to achieve our goals. With the power of positive thinking and gratitude, we can cultivate the self-discipline needed to reach our goals.

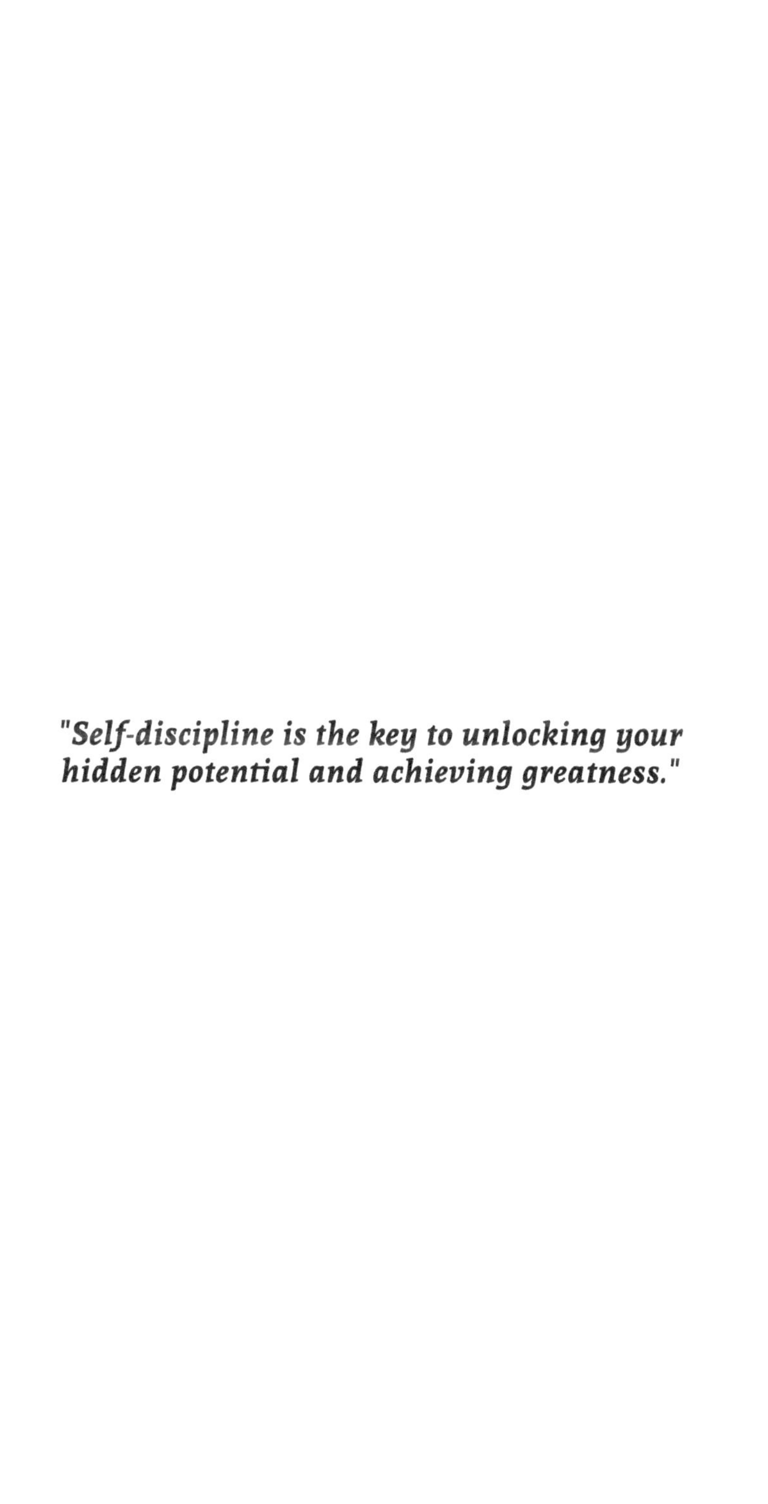

"Self-discipline is the key to unlocking your hidden potential and achieving greatness."

X

Dealing with Failure and Learning from Mistakes

Failure is an inevitable part of life, and it can be difficult to accept and learn from. However, it is important to remember that failure is not the end of the world. Instead, it is an opportunity to learn and grow.

The first step in dealing with failure is to accept it. It is important to recognize that failure is a part of life and that it is okay to make mistakes. Once you have accepted the failure, it is important to take the time to reflect on what went wrong and why. This reflection can help you to identify areas for improvement and to develop strategies for avoiding similar mistakes in the future.

The next step is to take action. Once you have identified areas for improvement, it is important to take action to address them. This could involve setting goals, developing a plan of action, and taking steps to implement the plan. It is also important to be patient and to recognize that progress may not happen overnight.

Finally, it is important to remember that failure is not the end of the world. Instead, it is an opportunity to learn and grow. It is important to take the time to reflect on what went wrong and to develop strategies for avoiding similar mistakes in the future. It is also important to take action to address areas for improvement and to be patient with yourself as you work towards achieving your goals.

By taking the time to reflect on failure and to take action to address areas for improvement, you can learn from your mistakes and use them as a stepping stone to success. Cultivating self-discipline and learning from mistakes can help you to achieve your goals and to live a more fulfilling life.

"Self-discipline is the key to unlocking your potential and achieving your goals."

XI

Building Resilience and Coping with Setbacks

Building resilience and coping with setbacks are essential components of cultivating self-discipline. When faced with adversity, it is important to be able to bounce back and remain focused on achieving your goals. This chapter will provide readers with strategies for developing resilience and managing setbacks.

Resilience is the ability to adapt to difficult situations and to remain focused on your goals despite the challenges. It is important to recognize that setbacks are a normal part of life and that they can be used as learning opportunities. Developing resilience requires a combination of self-awareness, self-care, and problem-solving skills.

Self-awareness is the first step in developing resilience. It involves recognizing your emotions and understanding how they affect your behavior. Self-care is also important for resilience. This includes taking care of your physical and mental health, such as getting enough sleep, eating healthy, and engaging in activities that bring you joy.

Problem-solving skills are also essential for resilience. This involves breaking down a problem into smaller, more manageable pieces and then developing a plan of action. It is important to be flexible and to adjust your plan as needed.

When faced with a setback, it is important to take a step back and assess the situation. It is also important to remember that setbacks are not permanent and that you can learn from them. It is important to focus on the positive and to take action to move forward.

Finally, it is important to remember that resilience is a skill that can be developed over time. With practice, you can become more resilient and better equipped to handle setbacks. By following the strategies outlined in this chapter, readers will be able to cultivate self-discipline and develop the resilience needed to cope with setbacks and achieve their goals.

"Self-discipline is the key to unlocking your inner power and achieving your dreams."

XII

Learning to Adapt and Be Flexible

In today's ever-changing world, it is essential to be able to adjust to new situations and environments. Being able to adapt and be flexible can help you to stay ahead of the curve and reach your goals faster.

Adaptability is the ability to adjust to new circumstances and environments. It is the ability to think on your feet and make quick decisions. Being able to adapt to new situations can help you to stay ahead of the competition and reach your goals faster. It can also help you to stay focused and motivated when faced with unexpected challenges.

Flexibility is the ability to adjust to different situations and environments. It is the ability to be open to new ideas and approaches. Being flexible can help you to stay ahead of the competition and reach your goals faster. It can also help you to stay focused and motivated when faced with unexpected challenges.

Learning to adapt and be flexible is an important part of cultivating self-discipline. It is essential to be able to adjust to new situations and environments in order to stay ahead of the competition and reach your goals faster. Adaptability and flexibility can help you to stay focused and motivated when faced with unexpected challenges.

By learning to adapt and be flexible, you can stay ahead of the curve and reach your goals faster. You can also stay focused and motivated when faced with unexpected challenges. Cultivating self-discipline through adaptability and flexibility can help you to stay on track and reach your goals. With the right mindset and attitude, you can learn to adapt and be flexible in order to achieve your goals.

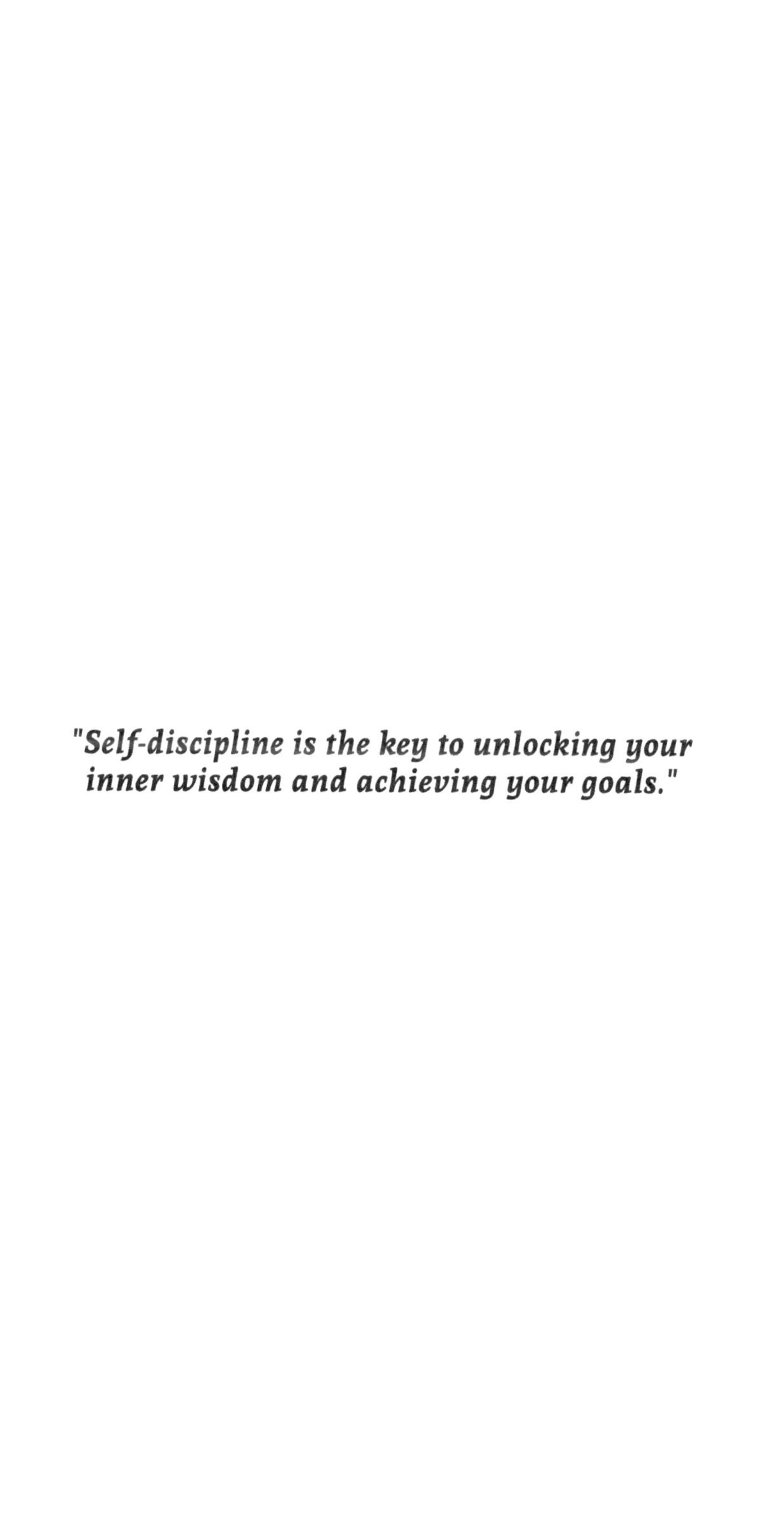
"Self-discipline is the key to unlocking your
inner wisdom and achieving your goals."

XIII

The Role of Mindfulness in Self-Discipline

Mindfulness is an essential tool for cultivating self-discipline. It is a practice of being aware of the present moment and accepting it without judgment. By being mindful, we can become more aware of our thoughts, feelings, and behaviors, and how they affect our ability to reach our goals.

Mindfulness can help us to become more self-disciplined by allowing us to recognize our triggers and patterns of behavior. When we become aware of our triggers, we can take steps to avoid them or manage them in a more productive way. For example, if we become aware that we tend to procrastinate when we are feeling overwhelmed, we can take steps to break down our tasks into smaller, more manageable chunks.

Mindfulness can also help us to stay focused on our goals. By being mindful of our thoughts and feelings, we can recognize when we are getting distracted and refocus our attention on our goals. This can help us to stay motivated and on track.

Finally, mindfulness can help us to develop a greater sense of self-compassion. When we are mindful of our thoughts and feelings, we can recognize when we are being too hard on ourselves and practice self-compassion. This can help us to stay motivated and focused on our goals, even when we make mistakes or experience setbacks.

Overall, mindfulness is an invaluable tool for cultivating self-discipline. By being mindful of our thoughts, feelings, and behaviors, we can become more aware of our triggers and patterns of behavior, stay focused on our goals, and practice self-compassion. With regular practice, mindfulness can help us to develop the self-discipline we need to achieve our goals.

"Self-discipline is the key to unlocking your inner courage and achieving your ambitions."

XIV

The Power of Persistence and Determination

The power of persistence and determination is a key factor in achieving any goal. It is the driving force behind success, and it is essential to cultivate self-discipline. Without it, our dreams and ambitions will remain just that - dreams.

Persistence and determination are the two most important traits for achieving success. They are the foundation of self-discipline, and they are the key to unlocking our potential. Persistence is the ability to keep going despite obstacles and setbacks. It is the ability to stay focused and motivated, even when the going gets tough. Determination is the will to keep pushing forward, no matter what. It is the strength to keep going, even when the odds are stacked against you.

These two traits are essential for cultivating self-discipline.

They are the fuel that drives us to reach our goals. They give us the courage to take risks and the strength to overcome any obstacle. They are the keys to unlocking our potential and achieving our dreams.

Persistence and determination are the cornerstones of success. They are the foundation of self-discipline and the driving force behind achieving our goals. They give us the courage to take risks and the strength to overcome any obstacle. They are the keys to unlocking our potential and achieving our dreams.

The power of persistence and determination is undeniable. It is the fuel that drives us to reach our goals and the foundation of self-discipline. It is the courage to take risks and the strength to overcome any obstacle. It is the key to unlocking our potential and achieving our dreams. Cultivating self-discipline through persistence and determination is the surest way to success.

"Self-discipline is the key to unlocking your inner resilience and achieving your aspirations."

XV

Important Things to be followed to achieve Your Goals

In order to achieve your goals, there are several key steps that must be taken. I will outline the main things to be followed in order to reach your desired outcome.

First and foremost, it is essential to set clear and achievable goals. This means that you must identify what you want to accomplish and create a plan of action to get there. It is also important to break down your goals into smaller, more manageable tasks. This will help you stay focused and motivated as you work towards your goal.

Second, it is important to stay organized and disciplined. This means that you must create a schedule and stick to it. This will help you stay on track and ensure that you are making progress towards your goal. Additionally, it is important to stay motivated and positive. This means that you must find ways to stay inspired and remind yourself why you are working towards your goal.

Third, it is important to stay focused and consistent. This means that you must stay focused on your goal and not get distracted by other tasks or activities. Additionally, it is important to stay consistent in your efforts. This means that you must be willing to put in the necessary work and effort to reach your goal.

Finally, it is important to be patient and persistent. This means that you must be willing to put in the time and effort to reach your goal. Additionally, it is important to remain patient and not give up when things get difficult.

By following these steps, you will be able to cultivate the self-discipline necessary to achieve your goals. With dedication, focus, and consistency, you will be able to reach your desired outcome.

"Self-discipline is the key to unlocking your inner determination and achieving your objectives."

ꙮ

OTHER BOOKS OF THE AUTHOR

1. The Moments When I Met God
2. Kashiyile Theertha Pathangal
3. GURU GYAN VANI
4. Abhiprerak Gita
5. ASSI SE JAIN GHAT TAK
6. Hopelessness of Arjuna
7. The Soul and It's True Nature
8. Sense of Action (Karma)
9. Action through Wisdom
10. Action through Wisdom
11. THEORY AND PRACTICAL OF EVERY ACTION
12. LOGICAL UNDERSTANDING OF THE SUPREME
13. THE IMPERISHABLE SUPREME
14. Yatra Nishadraj se Hanuman Ghat Tak
15. Yatra Karnatak Ghat se Raja Ghat Tak
16. Yatra Pandey Ghat se Prayagraj Ghat Tak
17. Yatra Ranjendra Prasad Ghat se Dattatreya Ghat Tak
18. YaatraSindhiya Ghat se Gwaliar Ghat Tak
19. Yatra Mangala Gauri Ghat se Hanuman Gadhi Ghat Tak
20. Yatra Gaay Ghat Se Nishad Ghat Tak
21. MAA GANGA, GHATEN EVM UTSAV
22. Ganga Arti Dev Deepavali evam Any Utsav
23. Potentials of Digitalized India
24. VEDIC CONSCIOUSNESS
25. A Brief Introduction to Vedic Science
26. Kashi ke Barah Jyotirling
27. IMPACT OF MOTIVATION
28. Let's have a Milky Way Journey
29. Color Therapy in a Nutshell

30. Rigveda in a Nutshell
31. Yajurveda in a Nutshell
32. Samveda in a Nutshell
33. Atharva Veda in a Nutshell
34. Ayushman Bhava - Ayurveda
35. Srimad Bhagavad Gita and Upanishad Connection
36. Srimad Bhagavad Gita - an attempt to summarize each chapter.
37. Facts and Impact of Nakshatra
38. Astro Gems - NAVARATNA
39. Ekadashi - A Concise Overview
40. A Concise View of Hanuman Chalisa
41. Inspirational Gita
42. Nakshatraranyam
43. Summary of 18 Mahapuranas
44. Synopsis of 18 Upa Puranas
45. Rigvediya Upanishads
46. Shukla Yajurvediya Upanishads
47. Krishna Yajurvediya Upanishads
48. Samavediya Upanishads
49. Atharvavediya Upanishads
50. The Seven Great Sages
51. From Rocket Scientist to President Dr. APJ Abdul Kalam
52. The Visionary's Voice - Quotes of Dr. APJ Abdul Kalam
53. The Wisdom of Swami Vivekananda: Insights and Inspiration from a Legendary Spiritual Teacher
54. Ayurvedic Remedies from the Garden
55. Sages and Seers
56. Rising Strong – Motivational Stories of Women
57. Beyond Flames -Mystery stories of Funeral Ghat Manikarnika
58. The Origins of Tulsi: A Look at the Mythological Roots of the Plant"

59. The Holistic Cow: A Look at the Physical, Spiritual, and Cultural Importance of Cows in India
60. Arts of Healing
61. Exploring the Divine
62. Understanding Five Elements
63. The Etymology of Ram
64. Symbols of India
65. Voice of Change (About Speeches of Great Men)
66. She Speaks (About Speeches of Great Women)
67. Patriotism on Celluloid – Brief About Patriotic Films
68. The Music of Motivation: A Brief Guide to Inspirational Film Songs
69. **Unlocking the Secrets of the Dashopanishads**
70. A Cultural Mosaic
71. Ancient Traditions, Modern Minds
72. Ecos of Ancient Wisdom
73. Beneath the Surface
74. From Temples to Ashrams
75. Sages of the Subcontinent
76. The Art of Healling (Ayurveda, Yoga & Naturopathy)
77. Indian Kitchen
78. The Festivals of India
79. The Indian Epics Retold
80. The Power of Mantras
81. The Indian River Ganges
82. The Indian Architecture
83. Rites of Passage
84. The Indian Silk Road
85. The Indian Literature
86. The Indian Villages
87. The Indian Folks & Crafts
88. The Way of Buddha
89. The Ramayan of Tulsidas

90. Astrological Remedies
91. The Secret Power of Motivation
92. Secret of Developing your Inner Strength
93. The Secret Path to Motivation
94. The Art and Secret of Positive Thinking
95. The Secrets of Practicing Ethical Living
96. Indian Art and Painting
97. The Indian Herbalism
98. Bharatanatyam to Kathak
99. Exploring India's Astrological Remedies
100. The Indian Festival of Flowers
101. Indian Handicrafts
102. The Splashes of Joy – India's Colour Festival
103. The Indian Science of Astrology
104. The Indian Mythology
105. Path to Enlightenment
106. The Indian Spirituality for Children
107. Aromas of India
108. The Secrets of Healthy Relationships
109. Ancestral Ties
110. The Indian Street Food
111. Discovering America
112. The Indian Textile
113. Listening to Motivational Speeches
114. Taste of India
115. A Cultural Journey through Indian Nuptials
116. Motivational Quote for Change
117. Secret Strategies for Making Money
118. Secrets to Cultivate a Positive Mindset
119. A Tapestry of Cultures: Exploring India from Kashmir to Kanyakumari
120. Achieving Your Dreams with Resilience: Secret Strategies for Overcoming Obstacles

121. Innovative Startups - 25 Startup Ideas to Spark Your Business Creativity
122. Export Management: Strategies for Global Success
123. Exporting from India - A Step by Step Guide
124. Finance Fundamentals: Mastering Financial Management for Business Success
125. Global Growth Strategies for International Business Development
126. Marketing Mastery: Unlocking the Secrets of Modern Marketing
127. Operations Mastery: Managing the Flow of Value in Business
128. Strategic Business Management: Navigating the Modern Business Landscape
129. Human Resource Management Strategies for Building and Managing a High Performance Team
130. The Indian Landscapes and Nature: An Exploration Of India's Natural Beauty And Diversity
131. The Indian Street Performances: A Cultural Exploration of India's Street Performances
132. Affirming Your Self-Worth: Strategies for Achieving Emotional Wellbeing
133. Cultivating Self-Discipline: Secrets Methods for Achieving Your Goals
134. Embracing Change: Strategies for Adapting to Life's Challenges
135. Embracing Your Uniqueness: Secret Strategies for Living an Authentic Life
136. Finding Motivation in Despondency: Coping with Difficult Times

Contact

DR. JAGADEESH PILLAI

MBA & PhD in Vedic Science

Four Times Guinness World Record Holder

Winner of Mahatma Gandhi Vishwa Shanti Puraskar and Global Peace Ambassador

Gemology, Astro & Vastu Consultant - Spiritual Counselor

Consultant for designing World Record Ideas

Efficient Tarot Card Reader

9839093003

myrichindia@gmail.com

drjagadeeshpillai@facebook

drjagadeeshpillai@instagram
jagadeeshpillai@youtube

www. JAGADEESHPILLAI.com

|| LOKAHA SAMASTHAHA SUKHINO BHAVANTU ||

9 798889 593089

Printed by Libri Plureos GmbH in Hamburg,
Germany